OUTDOOR WOOD WORKS

WITH COMPLETE PLANS FOR TEN PROJECTS

Schiffer Publishing Ltd

Tina Skinner

4880 Lower Valley Road, Atglen, PA 19310

ACKNOWLEDGMENTS

This book was made possible by the Hickson Corporation, which supplied all the photos herein. The photographs were taken by the Hickson Corporation at the suggestion of builders and architects who used Wolmanized® pressure-treated wood, a brand-name product of Hickson.

I am especially indebted to Huck DeVenzio, who has organized and attended photo shoots for every kind of wood project imaginable, from a car bumper to a luxurious shopping area in Hawaii (tough job) and who has kept meticulous and extensive files.

Also, the project plans included in this book were developed for Hickson Corp.

Skinner, Tina.
    Outdoor wood works: with complete plans for ten projects / Tina Skinner.
        p.   cm.
    ISBN 0-7643-0446-1 (pbk.)
    1. Outdoor furniture. 2. Woodwork. 3. Garden ornaments and furniture--Design and construction. 4. Fences. 5. Building, Wooden. I. Title.
TT197.5.09S55   1998
684.1'8--dc21   97-40473
                                            CIP

Book design by Blair R. Loughrey

ISBN: 0-7643-0446-1
Printed in Hong Kong

Published by Schiffer Publishing Ltd.
4880 Lower Valley Road
Atglen, PA 19310
Phone: (610) 593-1777; Fax: (610) 593-2002
E-mail: schifferbk@aol.com
Please write for a free catalog.
This book may be purchased from the publisher.
Please include $3.95 for shipping.

Try your bookstore first.

We are interested in hearing from authors with book ideas on related subjects.

TABLE OF CONTENTS

INTRODUCTION

When settlers first came to the United States, they were able to push back the wilderness with strong fences made of native locust and chestnut, woods so resistant to rot and insect infestation that many have lasted even to this day. But blight took the chestnut, and man took much of the locust. So ingenuity had to step in and take over where Nature once provided.

The first widespread use of wood preservatives came in 1875, when pressure treatment with creosote was discovered as an effective preservative for railroad ties. The Industrial Revolution went full speed ahead, and soon utility poles, too, were being treated and erected everywhere.

In 1933, the CCA or chromated copper arsenate method of pressure treating wood was invented in India. It wasn't until the 1970s, however, that pressure-treated wood really caught on with American home builders and remodelers. Because it uses wood from plentiful, fast-growing trees, pressure-treated wood has made remodeling projects feasible for many homeowners.

Pressure treated wood has been put to a myriad of applications, from the shed out back to the mailbox post out front. The purpose of this book is to present an overview of possible projects, from small flower boxes to giant tree forts. There are project plans in the back for those who need a little guidance in sculpting their own masterpiece from the diverse, long-lasting lumber now available on the market. And there are more than a hundred and fifty pictures to help stir the imaginations of all who aspire to improve their homes.

Most brand-name lumber companies offer a lifetime warranty on their pressure treated wood, so with a little planning and a minimum of maintenance, your projects are sure to last for years to come.

Chapter 1

MAKING GOOD NEIGHBORS

KEEPING YOU POSTED

One of the earliest uses for wood outside of the home was fencing. Fences kept domestic animals in, wild animals out. New technology has made wood more affordable and long-lasting, so the functions of fencing have been expanded to include beautifying one's surroundings and staking out a larger share of privacy. Post and rail fencing is one of the earliest forms of fencing used in this country, and still beautiful in its simplicity.

Posts and rails were first formed from tree trunks and large branches that, once cut down, required little work to ready them for their role as barriers. Flat board fencing is a way of utilizing large trees and getting more fence from fewer trees.

New suburban communities didn't require heavy fencing able to withstand the weight of a cow or horse. Instead, they needed pretty fences to help showcase their small plots of land, as well as fences that helped keep pets inside, others' pets outside. Picket fences, pretty and relatively petite, became an idealized frame for suburbanites' dream homes. Plans for a picket fence are included on Page 103.

Natural wood picket fencing, as opposed to the standard, white-painted picket fence, creates a different feel, especially when contrasted with brick posts.

Rough-hewn "pales" with tapered ends create
a primitive picket fence with rustic charm.

Instead of a point on top, these thin, straight boards were beveled to sit flush with the top rail and form a fence that mimics the balcony railing above.

Tall, straight rails create a privacy screen
in this Pittsburgh, Pennsylvania, backyard.

Sans the arrow-shaped top, straight balusters take on
a different persona encircling a suburban backyard.

Many fences have a back and a front, and it is important to decide in advance which side will face you and which side will be looked at by the neighbors.

A scalloped top transforms these straight boards into
a fair imitation of their forebear, the picket fence.

The same technique looks different on this fence, where the boards are placed closer together before arches are cut along the top of each panel.

An arched top line is further enhanced by routed and beveled posts.

SHADOW BOXING

The two-sided problem is solved with this alternating-board design, called a shadow-box fence. Boards are offset on both sides of the railings to create an identical appearance on both sides of the structure.

A shadow-box fence allows some light to come through.

Notice the different effects created by a dark stain and a black wash. Also,
rounding the tops of the uprights creates a softer effect for this style of fence.

Solid board fencing has become popular in suburban
areas where people seek increasing privacy.

Interest was created here by cutting small notches at the tops of these wide, vertical uprights, and by allowing the posts to stand slightly highter than the board panels.

Varying board widths and a sawed-off-point effect on the wider boards make this fence stand out.

Again, varying board widths add appeal. Notice also that the board panels start more than a foot off the ground, raised as though on stilts.

A rich effect is created here with a board shelf on top of an upright-board fence. Also, heavy posts and a bottom rail complete the framed effect, and the draped-style gate contributes additional flair to this beautiful fence.

Painted upright boards top a low brick wall, framed by brick posts. An arched, lattice gateway completes this classic look.

Basket-weave fencing is another alternative for overcoming the good side/bad side syndrome of wood fencing. Here horizontal boards bend around the posts, create a curved effect, and allow strips of sunlight through while still assuring privacy for the occupants.

LATTICE TOUCHES

Lattice softens the effect of a tall, board fence. Lattice is both beautiful and practical, allowing sunlight to penetrate.

Notice how the effect differs with different lattice/board ratios. Also, framework and fancy post caps add luxuriance to the overall appearance. Plans for a similar fence are on Page 104.

White paint has a dramatic impact on lattice
and board fences, creating Victorian ambiance.

Fences made completely of lattice are another option for tall barriers, allowing softened views both in and out.

A short span of lattice fencing defines a
patio and creates a semi-private screen.

Here a short lattice fence takes over the role of picket fencing, outlining a front yard and providing a backdrop for stretches of flower beds.

Lattice can help assimilate chain-link fencing into a more natural environment.

Different looks can be achieved with lattice, using devices such as heavy framing as in this staircase, or softening effects such as this arched gateway.

33

A top rail can also contribute a different look to lattice fencing.

Chapter 2

RETAINING WALLS

THE TIES THAT BIND

Lumber first achieved longevity in the late 1800s when a process was invented that used creosote to preserve railroad ties. Those ties made their way into lawns and gardens, primarily for use in retaining walls. Now these timbers are available in a much neater form—pressure treated.

Above and opposite: Landscape timbers are the perfect size for forming steps, and real workhorses when it comes to holding back hills and making them more habitable.

In addition to their value in landscaping, timber retaining walls create outdoor seating.

Steep hillsides can be made more habitable with the use of pressure-treated lumber. Such retaining walls create dramatic landscapes.

Modern lumber yards have perfected the old ties, creating effects such as these interlocking timbers.

Like their predecessor, the utility pole, round treated timbers have also found their way into private landscaping projects.

STANDING UP
UNDER PRESSURE

Pressure-treating technology has allowed for the use of thinner boards in retaining-wall projects. Properly treated for ground exposure, pressure-treated lumber can withstand rot and insects for decades while holding back erosion.

The natural colors and textures of wood retaining walls
make them an esthetic addition to gardening projects.

Solid posts and horizontal and vertical boards
combine for a natural-looking retaining wall.

Chapter 3

PLANTERS AND RAISED BEDS

SIMPLE WOOD FRAMES

Because wood blends so naturally with plants, lumber is a natural choice when it comes to showing off one's foliage. Here a simple structure serves as plant stand.

WE HOPE THAT YOU ENJOY THIS BOOK. . .and that it will occupy a proud place in your library. We would like to keep you informed about other publications from Schiffer Publishing Ltd.

TITLE OF BOOK: _____

☐ hardcover
☐ paperback

☐ Bought at: _____
☐ Received as gift

COMMENTS or ideas for books you would like us to publish. _____

_____

_____

_____

Name (please print clearly) _____

Address _____

City _____ State _____ Zip _____

☐ Please send me a free Schiffer Arts, Antiques & Collectibles catalog.
☐ Please send me a free Schiffer Woodcarving, Woodworking & Crafts catalog
☐ Please send me a free Schiffer Military/Aviation History catalog
☐ Please send me a free Whitford Press Mind, Body & Spirit and Donning Pictorials & Cook books catalog.

Telephone: (610)-593-1777   Fax: (610)-593-2002   E-mail: Schifferbk@aol.com

SCHIFFER BOOKS ARE CURRENTLY AVAILABLE FROM YOUR BOOKSELLER

SCHIFFER PUBLISHING LTD
4880 LOWER VALLEY ROAD
ATGLEN, PA 19310-9717

A simple shelf design also acts as a
showcase for summer's blossoms.

Some people put their plants on pedestals.

49

Below and opposite top:
Modern technology allows wood to serve as a container for wet soil and invasive roots. Ground-resistant, pressure-treated lumber will withstand rot and mildew for years, making it an attractive choice for flower boxes. Oblong boxes such as these can serve on the windowsill or against walls and along edges of narrow porches, decks, and walkways.

An attractive flower box is made portable with a dowel handle.

Planters big enough for ornamental shrubs work as bookends to a bench.

A wide base and top give this planter a classical touch.

A wood planter provides a nice contrast to the stone and brick wall behind it.

A lattice panel forms a trellis above this planter.
Plans for this project are included on Page 105.

A ceramic ornament provides the
finishing touch for this planter box.

PART AND PARCEL

Frequently deck and home builders include planter boxes as part of their structures, making gardening more convenient for urban and suburban dwellers.

Flower boxes allow for neatly packaged foliage right beside a pool.

In addition to hosting plant life, this large planter provides a
place to lean or sit while enjoying a relaxing lakeside view.

Planter boxes help outline a patio and provide color.

Additional wood and a grid trellis create
a unique environment for a garden.

For the creative homeowner with little garden space, planters can
be built right onto the home to make room for some greenery.

SETTING SOME LIMITS

Wood can simply be used to define a garden's perimeters.

Standard wood edging can be bought ready to
use from lumber retailers and garden centers.

Boards are often used in gardens to separate planted areas from walkways, though this zucchini plant has obviously obeyed its own laws.

Raised beds help elevate plants closer to eye
level and make maintenance that much easier.

Raised beds also
make it easier to
create an area of rich
soil for plantings. The
soil doesn't get
packed down by foot
traffic and is
therefore easier to
maintain and weed.

SPECIAL PLANTER PROJECTS

A hot box, or cold box depending on where you hail from, is a specialized planter used to start seedlings in early spring. A glass top helps trap in heat during cold days while still allowing the sun to shine in.

A planter is combined with a bench. Plans
for this project are included on Page 106.

The ultimate planter—a custom-built deck surrounds a tree.

A customized work bench makes gardening easier.
Plans for this project are included on Page 107.

Chapter 4

SEATING

TIME OUT ON THE BENCH

Wood helps make the outdoors more habitable for man.
A simple wooden bench—rising above dampness, insects,
and cold—makes sitting outdoors more enjoyable.

A bench, in its most simple
form, is an outdoor resting
spot and a space-saving seat.

With the addition of a back, arms, and some fancy scrollwork,
a bench is transformed into the realm of furniture.

An interlocking network of small boards adds beauty to a backyard bench.

MORE REFINED STATES

The traditional Adirondack chair and a more simplified version are shown here. When the curves are removed, the chair becomes easier for the layman to build. Plans for the simplified Chattahoochee Chair are included on Page 108.

A more experienced craftsman can make wooden furniture that begs to be lounged in.

A swing fit for two sits sheltered from rain and noonday sun.

Nothing suits a summertime crowd quite as well as a picnic table. Plans for this project are included on Page 109.

Outdoor seating can be combined with other uses, such as storage.

A unique shelf unit comes in handy as a countertop at barbecue time.

Here a bench helps protect a tree and incorporate
it into a family's outdoor living area.

Chapter 5

PROTECTION FROM ABOVE

CENTRAL MEETING SPOTS

Once the domain of the wealthy, gazebos are an increasingly common site outside large estates. They act as garden centerpieces and as great places for quick escapes to the great outdoors. They are informal meeting places, with a feeling of seclusion, even on an open lawn.

Above:
Spindle balusters on the railing and decorative scalloped trim under the eaves contribute to the fairy tale atmosphere surrounding this gazebo.

Left:
Unique railings and a wood-shingled roof help this gazebo blend in with the surrounding grounds and patio.

Above and following two pages: Many lumber and home-improvement retailers sell gazebo kits. Though some assembly is required, most can be erected in less than a day by an experienced do-it-yourselfer and a few assistants.

SHADY CHARACTERISTICS

A gazebo-like effect is created by using slats over roof beams. Though it won't provide any rain protection, this kind of roof filters sunlight and keeps it cool down below.

Above:
A trellis roof also forms the perfect bower for climbing plants.

Right:
Here irregularly placed slats create a shady nook over a bench and another shady resting point along a garden walk.

Once matured, an overhead grid of slats and foliage combine for an Eden-like refuge.

Chapter 6

WALKWAYS

UNDER THE BOARDWALK

More than just ornamentation, wood can help you pass from Point A to Point B, and lure you to pause in between.

Above:
Wood treated for ground contact makes for a softer approach to home, replacing hard cement sidewalks.

Left:
Note how the different diagonals of the boards help punctuate shifts in elevation in this wooden walkway as it runs behind a house.

Above:
A wooden walkway ties home, garden, and driveway together.

Right:
An eaves-sheltered walkway provides a transition between home and garden.

85

A wooden walkway replaces the traditional
cement skirting around this built-in pool.

GOING THE DISTANCE

An elevated walkway provides a bird's-eye view of this garden. A narrow arbor above allows for hanging plants, so the greenery is at eye level as well.

A wooden walkway takes the pressure off a well-worn path between home and lake.

A rocky culvert would be difficult to cross without this wooden bridge and walkway.

A bridge invites passage from lawn to woodland paths.

89

Wood and cement can be combined in infinite
creative patterns for a pleasing walkway.

Parquet, sold by most lumber and home improvement
retailers, is a simple solution to walkway needs.

Chapter 7

MISCELLANEOUS

PLAYING AROUND

Outdoor play is essential to children, and those with room for a fort or a swing set are truly among the lucky.

The number of projects that can be built using pressure treated lumber are limited only by the imagination. And children's imaginations are limitless.

Animals also benefit from outdoor wood structures.

STRICTLY UTILITARIAN

Sheds are a quick and easy solution to storage
problems. For plans, see Page 110.

A shed can house tools for lawn maintenance, and toys for lawn enjoyment.

A wood shed keeps fuel dry for winter.

Mailboxes can be mounted on sturdy timbers and stand for years. For plans, see Page 111.

Lumber and lattice can help hide utility boxes, air conditioning units, and trash cans. For a prototype, see Page 112.

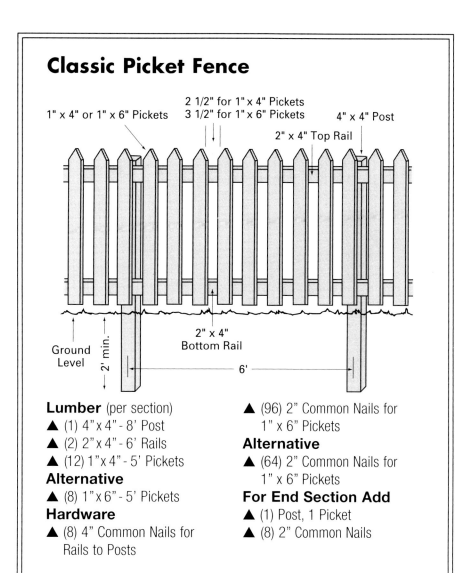

Classic Picket Fence

1" x 4" or 1" x 6" Pickets

2 1/2" for 1" x 4" Pickets
3 1/2" for 1" x 6" Pickets

4" x 4" Post

2" x 4" Top Rail

Ground Level

2' min.

2" x 4" Bottom Rail

6'

Lumber (per section)
- ▲ (1) 4"x 4"- 8' Post
- ▲ (2) 2"x 4"- 6' Rails
- ▲ (12) 1"x 4"- 5' Pickets

Alternative
- ▲ (8) 1"x 6"- 5' Pickets

Hardware
- ▲ (8) 4" Common Nails for Rails to Posts

- ▲ (96) 2" Common Nails for 1" x 6" Pickets

Alternative
- ▲ (64) 2" Common Nails for 1" x 6" Pickets

For End Section Add
- ▲ (1) Post, 1 Picket
- ▲ (8) 2" Common Nails

Privacy Fence with Lattice

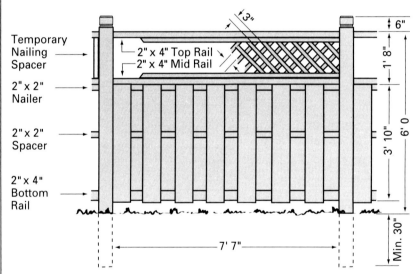

Temporary Nailing Spacer

2" x 4" Top Rail
2" x 4" Mid Rail

2" x 2" Nailer

2" x 2" Spacer

2" x 4" Bottom Rail

3"

6"

1' 8"

6' 0"

3' 10"

Min. 30"

7' 7"

MATERIALS
For approx. 8' section only.
First section includes 2 posts –
each additional section requires
one post.
▲ (2) pcs. 6" x 6" - 10'
▲ (3) pcs. 2" x 4" - 8'
▲ (2) pcs. 2" x 2" - 8'
▲ (5) pcs. 1" x 2" - 8'
▲ (1) pc. 2' x 4' Lattice
   cut to 17" x 91"
▲ (14) pcs. 1" x 8" - 4'

Gate (if required)
▲ (1) pc. 2" x 4" - 8'
▲ (1) pc. 2" x 4" - 12'
▲ (4) pcs. 1" x 8" - 4'
▲ Lattice if desired

Hardware/Miscellaneous
Concrete and gravel;
galvanized nails, hinges
and gate latch (if required);
semi-transparent or solid
stain as required

Planter Box

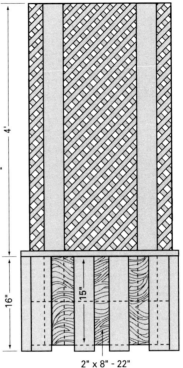

(2) 2" x 4" - 63"

2' x 4' Lattice

Lumber
▲ Base, Top Trim, Sides:
  (3) 2"x 4"- 12'
▲ Sides: (2) 2"x 4"- 8'
▲ Sides: (2) 2"x 8"- 8'

Hardware / Nails
▲ Base to Floor: 3"
  galvanized as required
▲ Sides 2"x 4" to 2"x 8": 2 1/2"
  galvanized as required
▲ Sides 2"x 8" to 2"x 8": 3"
  galvanized as required

Optional Lattice Work
▲ (1) 2'x 4' Lattice
▲ (2) 2"x 4" - 63"
  [(1) 2"x 4" - 12']

4'

16"

15"

2" x 8" - 22"

Box Front View

Top Trim

27"

1 pc. Lattice
2' x 4'

(2) 2" x 4" - 63"

2" x 4" - 23 1/2"

Base Top View

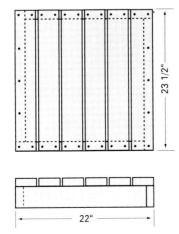

23 1/2"

22"

Base End View

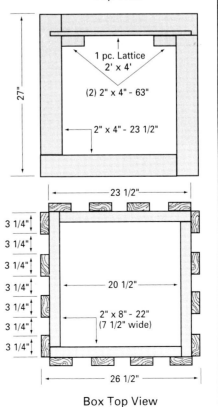

23 1/2"

3 1/4"
3 1/4"
3 1/4"
3 1/4"
3 1/4"
3 1/4"
3 1/4"

20 1/2"

2" x 8" - 22"
(7 1/2" wide)

26 1/2"

Box Top View

105

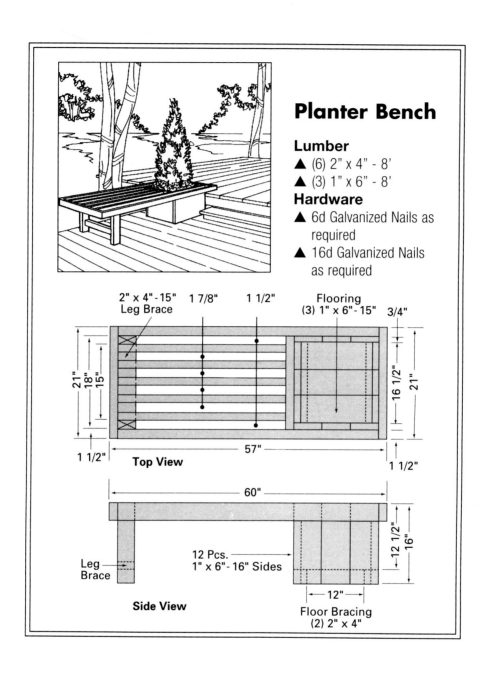

Planter Bench

Lumber
▲ (6) 2" x 4" - 8'
▲ (3) 1" x 6" - 8'

Hardware
▲ 6d Galvanized Nails as required
▲ 16d Galvanized Nails as required

Top View

2" x 4" - 15"
Leg Brace
1 7/8"
1 1/2"
Flooring
(3) 1" x 6" - 15"
3/4"

21"
18"
15"
16 1/2"
21"

1 1/2"
57"
1 1/2"

Side View

60"
12 1/2"
16"

Leg
Brace

12 Pcs.
1" x 6" - 16" Sides

12"

Floor Bracing
(2) 2" x 4"

Garden Work Bench

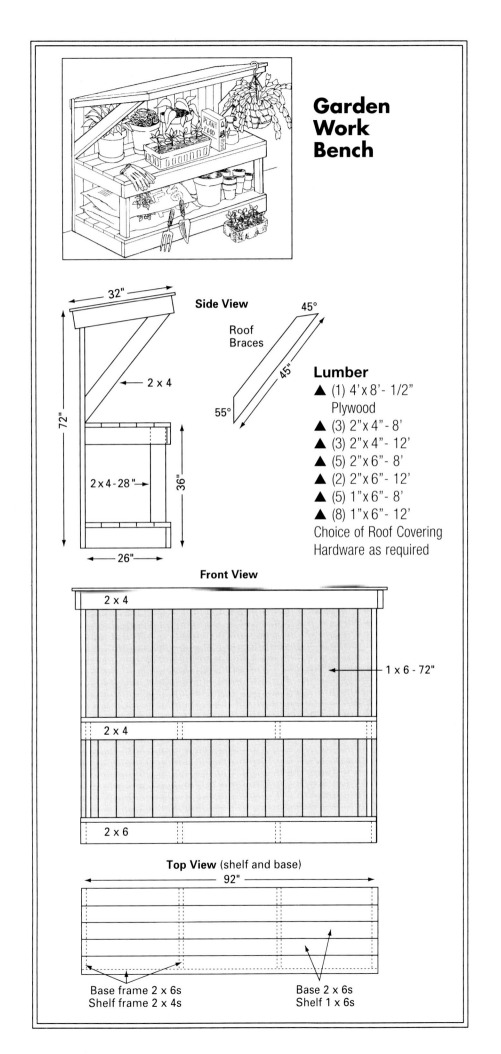

Side View

32"

72"

2 x 4

2 x 4 - 28"

36"

26"

Roof Braces

45°

45"

55°

Lumber

▲ (1) 4'x 8'- 1/2"
 Plywood
▲ (3) 2"x 4"- 8'
▲ (3) 2"x 4"- 12'
▲ (5) 2"x 6"- 8'
▲ (2) 2"x 6"- 12'
▲ (5) 1"x 6"- 8'
▲ (8) 1"x 6"- 12'
Choice of Roof Covering
Hardware as required

Front View

2 x 4

1 x 6 - 72"

2 x 4

2 x 6

Top View (shelf and base)

92"

Base frame 2 x 6s
Shelf frame 2 x 4s

Base 2 x 6s
Shelf 1 x 6s

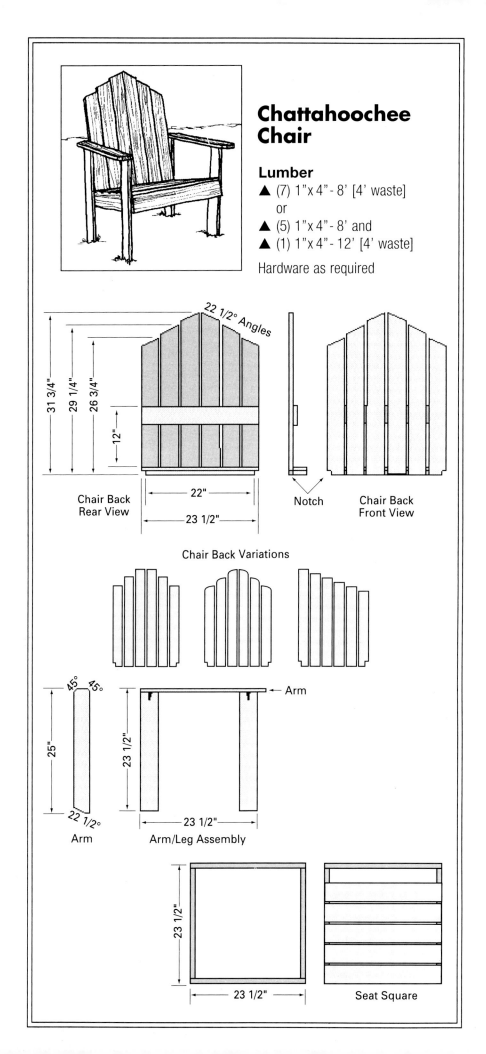

Chattahoochee Chair

Lumber

▲ (7) 1"x 4"- 8' [4' waste]
or
▲ (5) 1"x 4"- 8' and
▲ (1) 1"x 4"- 12' [4' waste]

Hardware as required

22 1/2° Angles

31 3/4"

29 1/4"

26 3/4"

12"

Chair Back Rear View

22"

23 1/2"

Notch

Chair Back Front View

Chair Back Variations

45° 45°

25"

22 1/2°

Arm

Arm

23 1/2"

23 1/2"

Arm/Leg Assembly

23 1/2"

23 1/2"

Seat Square

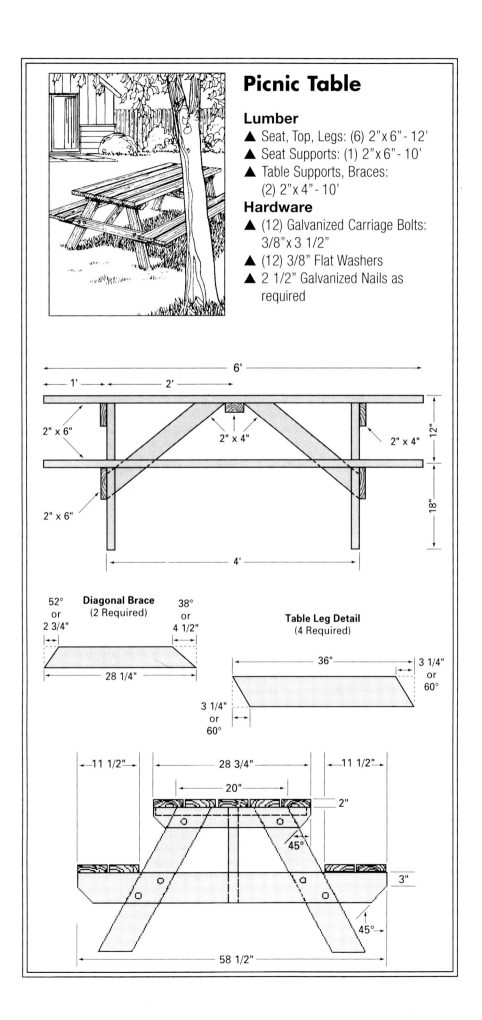

Picnic Table

Lumber
▲ Seat, Top, Legs: (6) 2"x 6"- 12'
▲ Seat Supports: (1) 2"x 6"- 10'
▲ Table Supports, Braces:
   (2) 2"x 4"- 10'

Hardware
▲ (12) Galvanized Carriage Bolts:
   3/8"x 3 1/2"
▲ (12) 3/8" Flat Washers
▲ 2 1/2" Galvanized Nails as
   required

6'

1'   2'

2" x 6"

2" x 4"

2" x 4"

12"

2" x 6"

18"

4'

Diagonal Brace
(2 Required)

52°
or
2 3/4"

38°
or
4 1/2"

28 1/4"

Table Leg Detail
(4 Required)

36"

3 1/4"
or
60°

3 1/4"
or
60°

11 1/2"   28 3/4"   11 1/2"

20"

2"

45°

3"

45°

58 1/2"

Storage Shed

Doors
Cut Double Doors from 2 sheets of 1/2" *Wolmanized* plywood and attach 1" x 4" *Wolmanized* trim as shown

Gable End Stud Detail
(2 Required)

-2' 4 1/4"-

End Stud Detail
(4 Required)

-1' 7 3/4"-
1 3/4" or 63°

6'9"

-2'6"- -2'6"-
5'

Rafters
Cut 14 rafters 6' 6 9/16" long from 2" x 4"s and nail to ridge beam blocks and ceiling joists

1 3/4" or 63° —— 6' 6 9/16" ——
1 3/4" or 63°

Ridge Beam Detail

Rafter Locations

—— 13' ——
-2'- -2'- -2'- -2'- -2'- -2'-
—— 12' ——

Ceiling Joists
Toenail seven 2" x 4" x 10' joists along side wall top plates with 10d nails

1 1/2" 1' 11 1/4" 2' 2' 2' 2' 1' 9 3/4" 1 1/2"

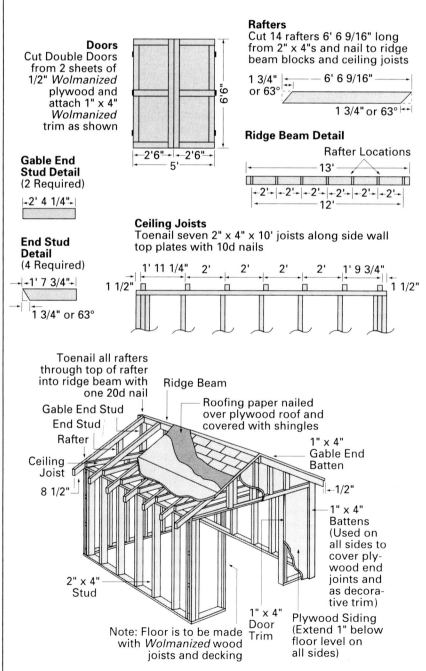

Toenail all rafters through top of rafter into ridge beam with one 20d nail

Gable End Stud
End Stud
Rafter
Ceiling Joist
8 1/2"

2" x 4" Stud

Ridge Beam

Roofing paper nailed over plywood roof and covered with shingles

1" x 4" Gable End Batten

1/2"

1" x 4" Battens (Used on all sides to cover plywood end joints and as decorative trim)

Plywood Siding (Extend 1" below floor level on all sides)

1" x 4" Door Trim

Note: Floor is to be made with *Wolmanized* wood joists and decking

Mailbox Stand and Planter

Lumber
Stand
▲ Post, Arm and Brace:
   (1) 4"x 4"- 12'
▲ Box and Planter Base:
   (1) 1"x 6"- 3'

Planter
▲ Sides, Ends and Bottom:
   (1) 1"x 6"- 4'

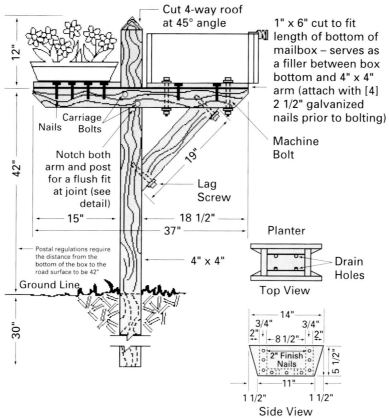

Cut 4-way roof at 45° angle

1" x 6" cut to fit length of bottom of mailbox – serves as a filler between box bottom and 4" x 4" arm (attach with [4] 2 1/2" galvanized nails prior to bolting)

Machine Bolt

12"

Nails

Carriage Bolts

Notch both arm and post for a flush fit at joint (see detail)

Lag Screw

19"

42"

15"

18 1/2"

37"

Postal regulations require the distance from the bottom of the box to the road surface to be 42"

4" x 4"

Ground Line

30"

Planter

Drain Holes

Top View

14"
3/4"   3/4"
2"   8 1/2"   2"
2" Finish Nails
5 1/2"
11"
1 1/2"   1 1/2"
Side View

Hardware
Stand
▲ Carriage Bolts with Nuts:
   (1) 4"x 4"- 12'
▲ Box and Planter Base:
   (1) 1"x 6"- 3'

Planter
▲ Sides, Ends and Bottom:
   (1) 1"x 6"- 4'

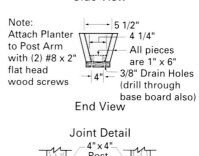

Note:
Attach Planter to Post Arm with (2) #8 x 2" flat head wood screws

5 1/2"
4 1/4"
All pieces are 1" x 6"
3/8" Drain Holes (drill through base board also)
4"

End View

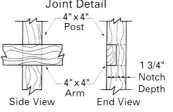

Joint Detail

4" x 4" Post

1 3/4" Notch Depth

4" x 4" Arm

Side View   End View

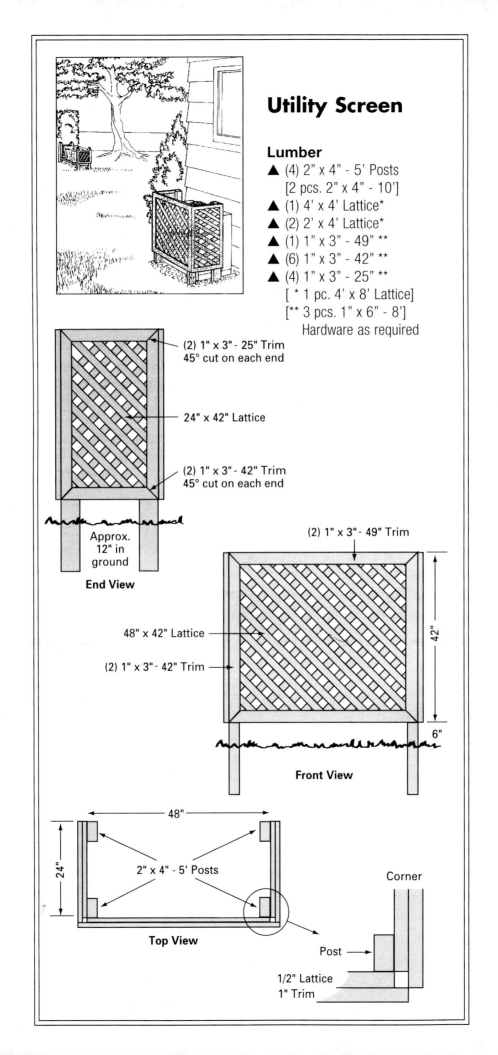

Utility Screen

Lumber

▲ (4) 2" x 4" - 5' Posts
   [2 pcs. 2" x 4" - 10']
▲ (1) 4' x 4' Lattice*
▲ (2) 2' x 4' Lattice*
▲ (1) 1" x 3" - 49" **
▲ (6) 1" x 3" - 42" **
▲ (4) 1" x 3" - 25" **
   [* 1 pc. 4' x 8' Lattice]
   [** 3 pcs. 1" x 6" - 8']
   Hardware as required

(2) 1" x 3" - 25" Trim
45° cut on each end

24" x 42" Lattice

(2) 1" x 3" - 42" Trim
45° cut on each end

Approx. 12" in ground

End View

(2) 1" x 3" - 49" Trim

48" x 42" Lattice

(2) 1" x 3" - 42" Trim

42"

6"

Front View

48"

24"

2" x 4" - 5' Posts

Top View

Corner

Post

1/2" Lattice
1" Trim